Of Earth and Timbers Made

Of Earth and Timbers Made

New Mexico Architecture

BAINBRIDGE BUNTING

Photographs by ARTHUR LAZAR

UNIVERSITY OF NEW MEXICO PRESS

Albuquerque

© The University of New Mexico Press, 1974. All rights reserved.
Manufactured in the United States of America.
Library of Congress Catalog Card No. 73-91766
International Standard Book Number 0-8263-0318-8
Designed by Dan Stouffer
First edition

*Thanks are due to the National Endowment for the
Arts, whose generous grant allowed me the time
and the means to complete work on these photographs.*

Arthur LaZar

CONTENTS

INTRODUCTION

This book is first and foremost a collection of photographic images. The photographer, Arthur LaZar, selected them from many hundreds of negatives made during innumerable weekend excursions over the past several years. Though he was obviously fascinated by the sculptural and figurative beauty of adobe buildings, this was by no means his only concern. In selecting subjects he was responding to images—to the beauty of shapes and textures and tonal values. He was not interested in structures for their historical importance alone, nor did he attempt to record the region's architecture in a systematic historical way.

With all of New Mexico as his province, Mr. LaZar seems to have been drawn instinctively to the Sangre de Cristo Mountains and the valleys adjacent to them. A geographical tally reveals that approximately half the plates show buildings on the south and east sides of the mountains—mostly north of Las Vegas—and half come from the western slopes including Taos and the Rio Grande Valley. Only three subjects are included from the Rio Abajo, the Rio Grande Valley south of La Bajada. The viewer may wonder why Indian buildings do not figure in this collection, especially when one considers the compelling beauty and historical importance of the pueblos. This omission is explained by the reluctance of the present-day pueblos to allow photography within their limits.

Although a short text accompanies each plate, the photograph can and should be studied and enjoyed independently. The images need no explanation or justification, as viewers with trained eyes will immediately see, and the text makes no attempt at any such explanation. Instead, it is conceived as a series of short essays concerned with the architectural or historical background of the subjects represented. In a sense these essays are an afterthought, the reaction of one viewer, delighted with the beauty and variety of the images, who also knows something about the area. The essays may be able to point out some interesting facts or details of which the reader was not aware, thereby adding a dimension to his enjoyment of the book. The pictures, however, come first; they are in no sense illustrations for a text. On the other hand, the plates have been arranged by topic. To some degree this sequence may illustrate the rich variety of architectural forms that developed in the area, and it may also facilitate comparisons between different eras of building activity.

The colonial architecture of New Mexico, it has frequently been pointed out, represents a fusion of native Indian and imported Spanish forms. The basic structure of earthen walls supporting a flat wooden roof is Indian, a tradition extending back for more than a thousand years. Though they lacked the technique of forming adobe into sun-baked bricks, Indians were capable of erecting structures of great size, as multistoried Taos Pueblo proves.

1

The Spanish adopted this basic structure. Their technique of forming the mud into bricks made construction more rapid, and the metal tools they brought facilitated the cutting and working of timber. Thus wooden doors and *portales* (porches), supported by *zapatas* (corbeled imposts) and posts, were added to the repertory of forms, as were fireplaces and outdoor ovens. They also brought the single-aisle church. But the great architectural contribution of the Spanish was the concept of large interior spaces. Metal axes made it practical to fell larger trees to use as roof beams, a change that resulted in more spacious living areas as well as big public enclosed spaces (churches) uninterrupted by supports. The traditional Indian room had been as narrow as seven feet; ordinary Spanish houses have a clear span of fifteen feet, churches as much as thirty.

Despite early Spanish innovations, few changes occurred after the Spanish settlement of New Mexico, and the technological capabilities of the area's inhabitants remained fairly rudimentary until the middle of the nineteenth century. For many communities mere survival was so difficult that little energy remained for technological innovation. Tools were crude and scarce, since they or the metal to make them had to be carted in from Mexico under extremely difficult conditions. For the same reason, window glass was unknown. Timber was plentiful, at least in the northern part of the province, but architectural elements made of wood were often crude and heavy for lack of adequate woodworking tools. It was easier to trim down a log with an ax to produce one structural member than to saw the log to produce two or more pieces of lumber. Thin boards for doors, windows, or trim were all but unknown. Architectural design also stagnated and, except for altar screens, reflected few of the changes that agitated Mexico during the eighteenth century.

Yankee influence began to penetrate the province with the opening of commerce over the Santa Fe Trail in about 1822, but it resulted in little architectural change for at least a quarter of a century. Along with new architectural styles, the Americans gradually reformed building technology. Sawmills processed posts, beams, and boards. The first such mill was established in Santa Fe by the U.S. army of occupation in 1848; a private mill began operation in Taos in 1852. Boards were especially important to the appearance of buildings, since they were used for trim and for various kinds of embellishment that had not previously been practical to fashion. In addition, traders furnished metal hardware and a steady supply of good tools to work the wood, and they introduced window glass for the first time.

Just how soon architectural fashion in New Mexico began to change is not clear. Construction dates for many buildings are unavailable, and many old structures have been remodeled. Because a building is known to have been built, say, in 1850, it by no means follows that its large windows and elaborate wood trim are part of the original design—a fact that several writers on New Mexican architecture have overlooked.

Along with sawmills, better tools, and window glass came a new fashion in architecture, the Greek Revival style. In East Coast centers this movement had begun as early as 1815, and it flourished in the South and Midwest before the Civil War. As the style spread to New Mexico, however, it was substantially changed as it adapted to the frontier economy and to adobe constructon. It is appropriate that this regional variation of the Greek Revival style is given a special name: the

Territorial style. First evident in trading and military centers like Santa Fe, Las Vegas, and Fort Union, the style spread gradually to outlying communities, and it may be said to have passed through two phases of development. The first, confined to the centers and moving along direct lines of communication, bears a recognizable relation to Greek Revival forms in the Midwest. The second phase is found in more remote villages, many of them located in the mountainous northern part of the state. Here the imported forms were elaborated on and subjected to minor changes and personal twists by artisans working in virtual isolation. Such variation on a common theme is the essence of folk art. The folk art that flourished on the New Mexican frontier is the subject of many of the photographs in this book.

The first phase of the Territorial style made little headway before the end of the Civil War (though this chronology requires investigation), and after 1880 it was submerged in the flood of Yankee tastes and practices that came with the railroad. The second phase flourished from about 1880 to World War I, a generation after the first phase. Its demise resulted from the improved communication that brought the largely self-sufficient villages into contact with and dependence upon the mainstream of American life.

The buildings of early New Mexico are today fast disappearing. The reasons for this are many: the economic stagnation of northern agricultural communities, the transitory nature of adobe construction and the ease with which it can be modified, and the impact of modern tastes and building practices. It is often observed that an adobe building neglected for a generation will have disintegrated beyond the point of repair. Given the ups and downs of almost any family plus the Spanish custom of dividing a dwelling among heirs, it becomes clear why so few of these buildings survive.

Today—as in 1880, as throughout recent history—no housewife will put up with an old kitchen or parlor if more up-to-date and comfortable solutions are available. Hence picture windows or wretched things of aluminum are now being substituted for old windows with wooden muntins, ill-fitting shed roofs are built on top of flat ones, and cement plaster of harsh grey replaces soft adobe. Worse still, shiny mobile homes are wheeled in and the old houses are converted to storehouses or barns or allowed to melt away completely. The change is already so complete that the history of the early New Mexican dwelling, if it is ever written, will have to be illustrated with photographs taken by an earlier generation.

1 Chacón Valley

Broad mountain valleys such as this one are the settings for about one-third of the buildings pictured in this book. This particular photograph shows the northern end of the Mora Valley occupied by the dispersed community of Chacón, on the eastern side of the Sangre de Cristo range. The floor of the valley is pasture, with an occasional field under cultivation; its sloping sides are wooded.

The valley lies within the bounds of the enormous Mora Grant, made in 1843 by the Mexican governor of the province to Cornelio Vigil, Ceran St. Vrain, and others. Far from the protection of the presidio in Santa Fe and open to incursions of Plains Indians, the area attracted few farmers before the establishment of Fort Union in 1851, though a settlement had been made in the Cleveland area in the early part of the century. The farms are small, though one finds large cattle ranches at the extreme south end of the valley and extending east into the rolling prairie. The higher elevation at Chacón receives more rainfall, though even here provision has been made for irrigation. In more prosperous times, grain and sheep were the main products. Wool was exported to eastern markets from Las Vegas, forty miles to the south, and flour ground from the hard grain of the Mora Valley was famous throughout the Southwest. Indeed, this valley boasted that it was "the breadbasket of the West." The economy was also stimulated by the presence of Fort Union some twenty miles to the east over a low range of hills; the fort was maintained until 1891. The valley's peak of prosperity was reached during World War I.

The farms here were adequate to provide a comfortable, though largely self-sufficient, livelihood. By today's standards, however, they are marginal; much of the land has gone out of cultivation, and many houses are abandoned. In very recent years some holdings have been acquired for summer use by outsiders or by native sons who have moved to the city.

2　Plaza del Cerro, Chimayo

As late as 1850, many New Mexican communities still required a degree of fortification, which they achieved by consolidating structures around four sides of an open space. Buildings were contiguous, with doors and windows confined to the plaza side of each edifice and no openings in outside walls. In case of an emergency, livestock could be herded into the open areas, the gates closed, and the compound defended. Such fortified places were referred to as *plazas*.

The Plaza del Cerro, which had come into existence by 1760, is the sole remaining example in New Mexico of this type of urban arrangement. Although the gateways are gone, some corner buildings have disappeared, several structures have been rebuilt, and numerous glass windows have been added, this village preserves the effect of an early community. The chapel in the foreground was long maintained by the Ortega family as a private oratory; a detail of this building is seen in plate 20.

A crumbling ruin beyond repair, this venerable adobe conveys something of the fortified appearance of a large New Mexico hacienda of the eighteenth or early nineteenth century. If there were originally exterior windows, as appears to have been the case in this building, they were small and protected by means of wooden bars. Judging from the height of the lintel there may have been a second such window (now walled up) to the right of the main door. But this dwelling bears evidence of the ease with which adobe structures can be remodeled. The central door, which is now surrounded by a wooden frame, appears to replace an earlier double gate. (Evidences of the earlier opening are the longer lintel and breaks in the adobe masonry.) To the right are three more doorways. They were probably cut at a considerably later date, especially the two at the right end, which have wooden frames and moldings. Several of the openings were walled up, probably when the structure was converted into a cattle barn. The erosion of the wall at ground level is the fate of all neglected adobe structures. Undermined in this fashion on the outside, adobe walls generally topple outwards when they collapse.

Historical documentation about New Mexican buildings is extremely scarce, and generally no information at all exists about remodelings beyond the internal evidence contained by the edifice itself. Local tradition has it that this structure was erected in about 1780 by Juan Lucero.

6 Phoenix Ranch

Phoenix Ranch is one of the cattle ranches located on the prairie just east of the mountains. It is appreciably larger than most holdings in the mountain valleys. The main house, erected in 1864 for William Kroenig, a merchant and rancher who had emigrated from Germany seventeen years earlier, is characteristic of the large dwellings built on some of these ranches. Surrounded by an elaborate wooden veranda of two levels, this structure exemplifies the ideal mansion as conceived in New Mexico during the later nineteenth century.

The relation of the Territorial style to the Greek Revival is perfectly illustrated here. The hallmark of such work is the pedimented (triangulated) lintel over doors and windows and the use of moldings to embellish the tops and bottoms of squared posts in an attempt to suggest a classical column. The handsome front door with top and side lights is entirely correct by Greek Revival standards, and would have been completely acceptable in the South or Midwest before 1850. By the time the building was constructed in New Mexico, however, the style had been out of fashion in the East for almost two decades.

The external symmetry of the central door framed by pairs of windows explains the inner plan: a hall flanked by rooms of equal width. The substitution of a door with top light for one window is probably explained by the fact that it was needed to provide access to the kitchen or the ranch office. The rather square plan, two or three rooms deep, is noticeably different from the single file of rooms that characterized even large colonial dwellings.

A crumbling ruin beyond repair, this venerable adobe conveys something of the fortified appearance of a large New Mexico hacienda of the eighteenth or early nineteenth century. If there were originally exterior windows, as appears to have been the case in this building, they were small and protected by means of wooden bars. Judging from the height of the lintel there may have been a second such window (now walled up) to the right of the main door. But this dwelling bears evidence of the ease with which adobe structures can be remodeled. The central door, which is now surrounded by a wooden frame, appears to replace an earlier double gate. (Evidences of the earlier opening are the longer lintel and breaks in the adobe masonry.) To the right are three more doorways. They were probably cut at a considerably later date, especially the two at the right end, which have wooden frames and moldings. Several of the openings were walled up, probably when the structure was converted into a cattle barn. The erosion of the wall at ground level is the fate of all neglected adobe structures. Undermined in this fashion on the outside, adobe walls generally topple outwards when they collapse.

Historical documentation about New Mexican buildings is extremely scarce, and generally no information at all exists about remodelings beyond the internal evidence contained by the edifice itself. Local tradition has it that this structure was erected in about 1780 by Juan Lucero.

4   Juan José Sánchez Homestead, La Cueva

Though a few hardy souls ventured into the valleys and plains east of the Sangre de Cristo Mountains in the second quarter of the nineteenth century, it was not until after the establishment of Fort Union in 1851 that settlers were free of the threat of marauding Plains Indians. The Juan José Sánchez homestead is characteristic of the building that took place on the smaller farms a generation later.

According to David R. Sánchez, born in 1882, his father Juan José moved across the mountains from Peñasco to this property in 1880. He erected for his family a one-room log house (the unit in the center with a metal roof) that was plastered outside as well as in. Subsequently he built two additions: the two-room log structure to the left and a slightly higher one-room adobe to the right. From the beginning, the additions had ridge roofs

of board-over-board construction similar to that shown in plate 15. The original flat-roofed unit was presumably covered with corrugated metal at a much later date.

The last structure as completed was a typical New Mexico dwelling with rooms arranged in a line, not all intercommunicating. Each of the five rooms contained one door or window on the sunny side of the building (in this case east); on the west were one window and one door. When the eldest Sánchez son was married in 1890, a three-room house (two more rooms were added later) was built at right angles to the early dwelling but not quite touching it (out of picture to the left), thus defining two sides of a courtyard. Log sheds, a barn, and, beyond that, corrals are seen to the right.

Juan Ortega House, Chacón   5

The Ortega family owned the most elaborate house in the upper Mora Valley. U-shaped, built around a garden that opens to the southeast, it is still characteristic of New Mexican dwellings built one room deep and without halls to facilitate movement between different parts of the house. It is unusual, however, in that its hillside location facilitated the construction of two stories in some sections. It was built late enough for the ridge roof and the elaborately framed doors and windows to have been parts of the original scheme. The first roof was of board-over-board construction.

From family tradition one learns that the house was erected about 1890, late enough for the family to have benefited from the railroad prosperity that affected the area and for the village to have developed its own individual variation of the Territorial folk art. The elaborate door and window frames (see plates 25, 34, 45) were the work of Aniceto Garduño, one of the most inventive of the village carpenters. Originally a veranda of two stories surrounded the wing in the foreground, and, at a single height, it was carried around the courtyard as well as across the left elevation.

6   Phoenix Ranch

Phoenix Ranch is one of the cattle ranches located on the prairie just east of the mountains. It is appreciably larger than most holdings in the mountain valleys. The main house, erected in 1864 for William Kroenig, a merchant and rancher who had emigrated from Germany seventeen years earlier, is characteristic of the large dwellings built on some of these ranches. Surrounded by an elaborate wooden veranda of two levels, this structure exemplifies the ideal mansion as conceived in New Mexico during the later nineteenth century.

The relation of the Territorial style to the Greek Revival is perfectly illustrated here. The hallmark of such work is the pedimented (triangulated) lintel over doors and windows and the use of moldings to embellish the tops and bottoms of squared posts in an attempt to suggest a classical column. The handsome front door with top and side lights is entirely correct by Greek Revival standards, and would have been completely acceptable in the South or Midwest before 1850. By the time the building was constructed in New Mexico, however, the style had been out of fashion in the East for almost two decades.

The external symmetry of the central door framed by pairs of windows explains the inner plan: a hall flanked by rooms of equal width. The substitution of a door with top light for one window is probably explained by the fact that it was needed to provide access to the kitchen or the ranch office. The rather square plan, two or three rooms deep, is noticeably different from the single file of rooms that characterized even large colonial dwellings.

7   Romero-Salman Ranch, La Cueva

Less than twenty-five miles from Phoenix Ranch is the old Romero Ranch, today owned by William Salman. The first owner of the property was Vicente Romero who obtained almost 30,000 acres from the old Mora Grant. The Romeros sold the property about 1869 to Duall and Lowden, British investors who had come to the Wild West to make their fortunes; they retained the property until 1919.

Begun as a traditional adobe of single-file plan, the dwelling was later enlarged with another story, and a two-level porch—that requisite of a fine mansion in New Mexico—which was added across the front. More recently, the house was doubled in width and the porch railing replaced with cast iron balusters. Inscribed on a stone set in the wall at the second level is "April th 2, 1863. B.R."—internal documentation of a sort that is all too rare in New Mexican buildings. Tradition has it that the carpenter who worked on the house came from Fort Union.

Los Luceros is another of New Mexico's finest haciendas, built of adobe and surrounded by verandas on two stories. Although the porches, as well as much of the interior trim, retain characteristic Territorial detailing, doors and windows were unfortunately changed when the building was renovated about 1925. The unusually good state of preservation of this important building is explained by the care that it has received as the home of some important art patrons and collectors: Miss Mary Wheelwright, who founded the Museum of Navajo Ceremonial Art, and Mr. and Mrs. Charles Collier, who established the Instituto Internacional de Arte Colonial Ibérico and endowed it with their fine collection of Spanish Colonial paintings.

The dwelling at Los Luceros is undoubtedly of some antiquity. It is said to occupy the site of a Pueblo ruin, and the lower parts of some walls may go back to the eighteenth or even the seventeenth century. But the present plan (three rooms deep on each side of a central hall) and external appearance (the double veranda constructed with mill-sawn timbers) clearly derives from the last third of the nineteenth century. Because of the ease and the frequency with which adobe structures can be modified, it is desirable to distinguish between the date at which a building might have begun and that from which its present appearance derives.

9   Mills-Clegg House, Springer

The two-storied mansion surrounded by verandas retained its prestige even after architectural styles began to change with the arrival of new fashions from the Midwest. This is demonstrated by the Mills-Clegg house, built in 1880 by M. W. Mills, who had made a fortune as a frontier lawyer. The house was erected after the railroad reached Springer, a fact that explains several of its architectural features.

The mansard roof undoubtedly caused a sensation on the frontier and symbolized the progress the territory hoped to achieve now that it was linked by railroad to the States. Already at this time in eastern centers, however, the mansard roof,

which had been in use since the mid-fifties, was passé. Instead of being sheathed with slate according to the eastern practice, the mansard here is covered with sheets of metal pressed in a design that simulates slating. Through technological innovations like these, Americans attempted to cut construction costs. Such metal sheeting, as well as the large plates of window glass, would have been very difficult to transport to Springer before the advent of the railroad.

Thanks for the careful preservation of this important landmark are due Mr. and Mrs. Luke Clegg, who purchased the property in 1937. Other views of the building are seen in plates 29, 36, 43.

Ruined Building, Arroyo Seco   10

This decaying house, in which adobe walls are literally dissolving, could be found almost anywhere in New Mexico. It explains why the area retains so few old structures in anything like their original condition even though men have been constructing homes in this region for more than a thousand years.

Walls made of sun-dried adobe (a combination of clay and sand) are prone to erosion, and roofs (wooded members supporting a heavy layer of earth) are subject to rot. Both walls and roofs require never-ending attention. At frequent intervals the walls must be reinforced at the ground line (see plates 3, 16, 52); the traditional way to repair a roof is to pile on another bucket or two of mud wherever it leaks. In this manner enormous roof loads build up over the years, and the moist earth causes the wooden covering to decay. As a rule of thumb, it can be said that roofs have to be replaced every 75–100 years. In a very literal sense this is "organic" architecture, subject to birth and decay. Neglect an adobe structure for twenty years, and it will have deteriorated to the point where it is not worth repairing. This is why structures like Phoenix Ranch and Los Luceros are so rare and important.

11   Roof Tops, Cordova

The basic adobe building is very simple: walls constructed of sun-dried brick supporting a flat roof of wood rendered reasonably watertight by a layer of earth. Traditionally the wood roofing members are level; slope is achieved by grading the earthen covering to a low point where a waterspout or *canal* is located.

Walls are usually carried above the roof to form parapets; thus the plan is evident when viewed from above. This house illustrates the traditional Spanish colonial plan with rooms arranged in single file. Sometimes, as here, the row will break to form an **L**, or, in the case of unusually large houses, it will continue around to form sides of a hollow core, the *placita*.

The Rio Grande Valley was settled more than two centuries earlier than areas on the opposite (eastern) side of the Sangre de Cristo range. Although located on the bank of the Rio Grande and on the main highway that today leads from Santa Fe to Taos, Pilar was not on the old route connecting these centers. Indeed, it was quite inaccessible from the south because of the sheer walls of the gorge in which the village is located, and the community was approached from the outside world by way of Taos. The original Spanish highway left the Rio Grande Valley at Embudo, nine miles south of Pilar, and made its way over the mountains to Taos by way of Dixon, Picuris, and Talpa; from Taos one would backtrack seventeen miles to this hamlet.

Although obviously deteriorated, with some buildings entirely destroyed, the arrangement of a block of houses like the one shown here suggests the plazas of the early fortified towns. Pilar, in fact, had two plazas, the smaller of which is pictured here. This plaza is a typical collective facade dating from around 1900.

With the exception of the low horizontal windows of the nearest section, which are clearly of more recent date, each door or window (in one case a very small window adjacent to a door) gives access to a different room, as is typical of New Mexico houses. In this row there are eight rooms.

13 Upper Morada, Arroyo Hondo

A morada is a meeting place for Penitentes, a group of laymen banded together to pursue spiritual ends. Because their religious practices, including self-flagellations, seemed extreme to churchmen sent to New Mexico by the Catholic church following American annexation, the Penitentes were officially discouraged. This drove the group into isolation and secrecy, a fact reflected in the design and location of their meeting places.

Adobe buildings traditionally were plastered outside as well as in with the same mud used to make the unfired brick for the walls. Originally there were very few openings in the walls because of the threat of marauding Plains Indians and the absence of window glass. The structure therefore appeared as a solid object, a piece of sculpture. This effect was enhanced by the eroded, rounded edges of the parapets and the irregular, undulating surfaces of the masonry.

The numerous windows required by our modern habits of living destroy the sense of the building as a solid, geometric object. This is why so many recent copies of traditional adobe houses miss their visual mark.

For other moradas, see plates 17, 21, 47, 63, and 64.

The sculptural character of an adobe building is often accentuated by buttresses that add a strong plastic quality. Such buttresses are generally not part of the original fabric but were added to reinforce a corner or a wall weakened by erosion. The buttress pictured is on the church of San Agustín at Isleta Pueblo, but the same form can be found on buildings in many parts of New Mexico.

In recent decades it has become usual to substitute cement plaster for adobe, though this hard surface lacks the soft beauty and texture of the natural material. Hard plaster eliminates the need to resurface the exterior walls with mud plaster every few years. But such a surface also has several disadvantages. When it cracks, moisture gets into the apertures and runs under the plaster crust, concentrating the erosion in certain areas. But because this is not evident on the surface, serious damage to the fabric often goes undetected for too long a period. The surface pictured here illustrates the point. Indeed, a large chunk of the front wall of the church simply slumped out of place during the winter of 1972–73.

15   Encarnación Trujillo House, Talpa

With the arrival of Yankee traders, who came in increasing numbers after the Civil War, building technology changed rapidly. One innovation was the introduction of sawmills that could produce an abundance of thin (one-inch) boards. Boards had been a luxury up to that time, since it was usually easier to dress down a piece of timber to the desired thickness with ax and adz, or to split it, than to cut it with the clumsy saw.

One of the first uses to which milled lumber was put was to make roofs, until then a source of perpetual trouble. Thin boards, laid with the slope, were placed contiguous to one another, with a second layer staggered to cover the joints. Usually the pitch was fairly steep, perhaps five inches in twelve. Such roofs were good at deflecting rain, but they provided no insulation. Often a new board roof was simply built over the old, flat, earth roof, in order to combine the advantages of each.

Roofs such as this one were built in mountainous areas where lumber was plentiful and where distances from the railroad made it unfeasible to cart in metal roofing. Even though they were not employed in Santa Fe or in Rio Abajo, roofs like these are a legitimate feature of Territorial architecture.

Archway, Severino Martínez House, Taos   16

Wood-hinged doors were so complicated and metal hinges so scarce that doors were sometimes omitted in early houses where one would expect them. An instance is this passageway of the Severino Martínez house, begun before 1832, which leads from the *placita* to the *corrales* contiguous with the rear wall of the house. A door was omitted in this critical location despite the fact that the owner was probably the wealthiest Taos merchant of his time who sent wagon trains to trade in Chihuahua. Similarly, the openings between rooms in some early houses were without swinging doors; the opening would instead be closed with skins or woven hangings.

Careful observation will show, however, that this opening is not closed by a structural arch. In place of the ring of voussoirs that would ordinarily deflect the weight of the wall, one sees adobe bricks set in a regular horizontal position, capable of supporting nothing and held in place only by the adhesive power of dried mud. It is interesting that arch construction was never exploited in New Mexico though it had been known in the region as early as the construction of the second mission church at Pecos Pueblo, in the early eighteenth century. The concrete foundations, which can be seen in the picture, were added in 1946 when an attempt was made to stabilize the decaying building.

17 Door to Chapel, Upper Morada, Arroyo Hondo

When doors were employed they were often heavy and surprisingly low. Though the present example dates from as late as 1852–56, it follows a familiar tradition. Despite a height of only 4 feet 10 inches, the framing members (vertical stiles and horizontal rails) of this door are over 2 ½ inches thick. Planks used to fill the panels are 17 inches wide and more than an inch in thickness. Although the framing members are hand planed, their surface is somewhat rough. The panels are quite irregular, with exposed adz marks and grained areas where wood has been split; beveled edges on the opposite face of the panels are made with an adz. Such clumsy timbers, shaped by hand, were employed in the absence of thinner, more workable boards cut at a sawmill.

The most interesting aspect of the door is the way it hinges on pintles, peglike extensions of one vertical framing stile. Because the pintles fit into sockets sunk in the sill and the lintel, such a door had to be hung before the lintel was fixed in place and could not be removed without demolishing the wall. The pintle is an ancient hinging device, known to have been used in Mesopotamia and Egypt. In New Mexico pintles were employed in place of metal hinges because of the cost of importing iron from Mexico. In local circles, a door hung on a pintle is referred to as a *zambullo* door, a term not much employed in Mexico. Simple leather thongs serve as door pulls.

On the right stile is carved a design resembling an inverted **R** which was explained by a local resident as standing for *"religioso"* and hence suggesting a sacred place. Appropriately, this design occurs on the chapel side of the door. Whitish earth pigment is applied to framing members and used for the cross design painted on the upper panel. The base of the cross is framed by a rectangle—perhaps a simple attempt to suggest perspective? A comparable cross on the reverse surface is animated by three parallel horizontal lines carved in its base. Plates 21a and b show other doors with crosses in this same building while other views of the building appear on plates 13 and 47. The wooden baseboard and floor were installed when the morada was remodeled as a residence; the original floor was packed earth.

Although they were necessary features of seventeenth- and eighteenth-century haciendas or fortified villages, very few gates like these have survived. The gate closed the zaguan, the covered passageway leading into the open courtyard or plaza. Usually the zaguan was wide enough to admit an oxcart. In early structures built to withstand Indian assaults, this stout gate was often the only opening in the external wall.

The gate shown here is unique among surviving examples because of its splendid iron hinges. In early New Mexico, imported iron was almost enough to rank as a semiprecious metal. The will of Severino Martínez, drawn up in 1827, divided bars of iron among the heirs as the wills of rich men of other eras might have distributed silver ingots. Though similar in design to Mexican examples, these beautifully shaped hinges were probably forged in Taos. The present doors are made of two layers of 1 5/16 inch boards—the outer vertical, the inner horizontal—secured by some 500 hand-forged nails. As in Mexico and Spain, one leaf of the heavy gate contained a wicket for pedestrians.

We cannot be certain when the Long house was built. Although tree-rings date vigas in some parts of the house (but not that which contained the zaguan) as early as 1816, Long did not arrive in Taos until 1839. On the other hand, such a building might predate the time of Long's residence by several generations, and traditions says that a fort once existed in the neighborhood. Today, however, the building has melted away almost entirely, and these fine gates have been reinstalled in a house near Albuquerque.

19   Paneled Door, Pablo Sena House, San José

This paneled design reflects Yankee antecedents rather than Spanish colonial. It imitates the four-panel doors produced commercially in the Midwest and East during much of the nineteenth century. Until the extension of the railroad to New Mexico, it was impractical to haul in such factory-made millwork. Instead, doors and windows were made by hand in the community in which they were to be used. Even moldings like those framing the panels were produced locally; a different knife and hand plane was used to create each profile.

As no structural explanation exists for the different widths of the stiles and panels on the upper and lower levels of this door, one must put it down to the artistic preference of the craftsman who built it. Perhaps he fancied the effect of large panels above, smaller ones below, but if this was the case his subtlety was lost on the hack who rehung the door upside down in its present location.

Entrance, Ortega Oratorio, Plaza del Cerro, Chimayo   20

A door like this one, with panels above and diagonal sheathing below, might be considered transitional between the doors pictured in plates 19 and 21. Despite their appearance, it is clear that the panels here were never intended to contain glass—which was still very scarce when the chapel was remodeled in the late nineteenth century—because the inner layer of vertical boards can be seen inside the panels. One edge of each of the framing members and both edges of the diagonal boards are molded with the same hand plane. This adds a subtle accent, while a heavier bead molding is used on the outer perimeter of the door and around the two panels. The exterior of this chapel is seen in plate 2.

The left detail illustrates an elaborate door combining diagonal boarding and panel designs. Four hand planes, each with a different profile, were needed to produce the variety of moldings used here, and the cross superimposed on the surface undoubtedly indicates that the door was made for a morada or private oratory. Now incorporated in the former morada at Arroyo Hondo,

the design of the door suggests that a mountain village like Truchas was its point of origin.

The design to the right, colored a deep red, is partially obscured by overpainting with white earth pigment. All the doors in this morada have crosses painted on both faces (plate 17). Interior doors were seldom built with a double layer of boards.

22   Lucero Store, Chacón

Of later date, these doors, from a store built about 1892, were equipped with glass panes. But even at that late date, some doors were still handmade. The carpenter here had an instinctive sense of proportion, and both the pedimented lintel and the molding along the porch beam are nicely detailed. Oil paints came into use as commerce over the Santa Fe Trail increased; however, a coat of yeso (gypsum) was used to whitewash adobe walls owing to a longstanding custom in the area. Board-over-board roofs have been discussed previously (see plate 15).

This grass-roots example of a Territorial doorway makes an interesting contrast with the *portal* at Phoenix Ranch (plate 6). The ill-proportioned door and the lack of coordination between the frames of top and side lights suggest the work of a provincial carpenter who did not understand the shapes he was copying. The composition also lacks the pleasant accents furnished by a capping molding over the lintel or by panels in the soffit of the door.

Seen also in plates 32 and 33, this dwelling is essentially a single-file colonial house of adobe brought up to date with Territorial trim for doors and windows as well as a Territorial *portal* with squared posts.

24   Doorways, Las Vegas

On the left is the entrance of the Presbyterian church built in Las Vegas in 1871. The surer proportions and the way the paneling of the soffit and the reveals relate to the doors demonstrate that the carpenter responsible for this work knew his business. Indeed, the attenuation of the upper panels of the door reflects the elongated propor-

tions that characterized American architecture generally in the 1850's.

The face of the door frame resembles a classical aedicule with the vertical members capped with moldings recalling pilasters, the lintel suggesting an entablature. The makeshift dentil course was composed by sawing molding into sections and

nailing the sections at short intervals to the frame. In keeping with this somewhat sophisticated handling of details was a two-story portico, which added dignity to the facade. This seems to have been the only attempt to reproduce a temple front in New Mexico, though the Greek Revival style had produced many such features in the East.

The house door on the right falls somewhere between the "civil" proportions and detailing of the church *portal* and the folk art style found in entrances to houses in the mountain villages. Though proportions are clumsy, the robust bead moldings employed for the stiles and rails add a certain finish to the design.

25   Juan Ortega House, Chacón

One of the most charming chapters of New Mexico's architectural history concerns the folk art that developed in small communities about 1880 as carpenters worked out their own variations on motifs found in the Territorial style. As in all folk art, very few innovations were radical yet each had something individual. For this movement to flourish, an abundant supply of sawn lumber, good tools, and a fairly vigorous building program were necessary.

The names of most of those carpenters are forgotten but their individual traits are unmistak-

able once one begins to look for the differences. Aniceto Garduño woked in Chacón, a town sufficiently far from the railroad to encourage the use of homemade rather than imported doors and windows well into the present century. One characteristic of Garduño's work is his door design, where upper panels have a curious profile midway between a round arch and a pointed one. Such a design is undoubtedly a variation on that of the factory-made doors with roundheaded lights filled with glass that were so prevalent in the Midwest.

Auriano Martínez House, Llano de San Juan   26

A late but skilled practitioner of the folk art style was Alejandro Gallegos, who was active in the Rodarte area until his death in the 1920s. Characteristic of his work is the alternation of rectangular panels and ogee designs. In more elaborate commissions he also used a figure eight. The rectangular shapes are emphasized, yet the surrounding molding keeps them from being too heavy visual-ly. Gallegos also enjoyed complicated door frames employing splayed jambs such as those shown here, and sometimes he used a splayed doorhead as well. The construction of this two-ply door is essentially the same as that found at the Ortega *oratorio* (plate 20). This beautiful entrance was made for a simple adobe farmhouse of three rooms.

27   Storehouse Door, Los Luceros

Both this door and its frame are more intricate
than was usual, and the double row of dentils in
the frame and the star-shaped panels are without
precedent in the territory. Indeed, the panels,
compiled of eight pieces of diamond-shaped
wood, somewhat recall Yankee quilt designs. The
lower panel, however, forming a cross design,
repeats a pattern often found in the work of
Gregorio Ortega of Truchas, who did the splendid
double doors shown in the next plate.

These doors, the handsomest surviving from their era, are now used for the entrance of the chapel at Los Luceros, where they were installed in 1964. Originally, however, they were made, probably in the late 1870s, for the home of Policarpio Romero in Peñasco. The showplace of the Embudo watershed, this dwelling was largely demolished in 1936 to make way for a highway; it was totally obliterated in 1963.

According to oral tradition in Peñasco, the doors were the work of Gregorio Ortega, who came from Truchas. Here again the two-ply construction is elaborated with great ingenuity. All the shapes —cross, diamond, and square—are compiled with mitred sections of one type of hand-planed molding. The wooden casing of the deep-set door is unusually complex; both jambs and head are splayed. The cant of the lintel ends is unusually acute. The frame was originally closed with vertical facia.

29   Mills-Clegg House, Springer

This is a detail of the building seen in plates 9, 29, 36 and 43. The house, which combines a traditional two-story porch, surrounding the core, with a mansard roof, is clearly transitional. The same must be said of the ornamentation, which fuses pedimented Territorial door and window enframements with Queen Anne latticework. Although a bit simple and harsh by eastern standards, this complex wooden tracery clearly emulates the jigsaw work then popular in the Midwest,

as do the turned spindles set at different levels in the balustrade.

The railroad, which reached Springer in 1879, was essential to the construction of this house, built the following year. Without it there would have been little possibility of transporting so large a plate of glass as that used in the transom over the door. The house interior also contains doors, windows, mantels, and even the main stairway imported from the Midwest.

The early New Mexican house was devoid of the decoration so characteristic of Spanish colonial architecture elsewhere. There were no iron window screens like those found in Mexico, and no carved stone trim for entrances or cornices. If there was an element of architectural interest, it was a narrow *portal.* Here the beam running parallel to the facade was carried by *zapatas* (corbel brackets) supported by round posts. The front and back faces of the corbels were flat, though they might be animated by simple designs gouged out with a chisel; their profiles, combining scrolls and stepped designs, formed strong but simple outlines. Never was there relief carving as one finds in renaissance or medieval architecture. Ultimately the *zapata* traces back to the work of the Moors in Spain. In the example shown here, *zapatas* and beam are hewn from a single piece of wood sixteen inches deep.

31   Portal, José Maria Martínez House, Taos

Portales come in all degrees of complexity. This one is the simplest possible version: a crude construction of unshaped posts, beams, and rafters. But the fact that such a porch existed in the main patio of a Martínez house (the Martínezes were one of Taos's most prominent families) raises questions, as does the careless manner in which the top of the post was shaped to form a tenon to fit a mortice in the beam. Furthermore, this porch faces west, something that one almost never finds in New Mexico, where most *portales* are sensibly oriented to the east or south. All of this suggests that it may have been hastily constructed as a shelter when the empty house was converted into a cow barn.

Portal, Sándoval House, San Miguel   32

Although the wood trim is Territorial, the basic form of this *portal* is essentially unchanged from colonial times: it is a narrow porch, supported at intervals, extending along one side of a building. The only difference from a colonial *portal* is that these rafters, beams, and posts are squared, cut at a sawmill; also, sections of molding nailed to the top of the post have replaced colonial *zapatas*. Otherwise not much has changed: the walls, of adobe construction and adobe plaster, are covered with a thin layer of yeso, and the wooden roof carries a layer of earth "waterproofing."

33   Portal Detail, Sándoval House, San Miguel

This is a detail of the *portal* shown in the
previous plate. Note how all edges of the squared
timbers are accented by a hand-planed bead
molding. A classical capital is suggested by the
sections of molding with mitred corners nailed on
the four faces of the post.

34

Porch Details, Juan Ortega House, Chacón

Aniceto Garduño, one of the most original of
the folk carpenter-designers in New Mexico lived
until 1914. He could do wonderful things with a
saw, a brace and bit, a set of molding planes,
ample time, and plenty of good pine board.
Though the forms here are a long way from
Territorial shapes, the top of the column remains a
focus for embellishment. The inverted wave pattern imposed on the horizontal beam obscures its
structural function in a way no architect who
understood the Greek Revival style would have
countenanced.

35 Portal, Juan José Baca House, Socorro

Variations on the *zapata* capital are infinite, but this is one of the most fanciful. The carpenter sought to create a capital by combining bits and pieces of molding and complex cutouts. The most conspicuous elements of the composition were worked out as silhouettes cut from one-inch boards. Such details are not carved in a sculptural manner; if relief was desired, it was achieved by cutting still more silhouettes or bits of molding, and nailing them on the flat surface, as in plate 36.

Socorro was the boom town of the lower Rio Grande. At one point it was larger than Albuquerque; by 1890 it had a population of almost 5,000. A hint of its future prosperity came in 1867 when silver was discovered in the mountains west of the city, but until the Apaches were brought under control in the early eighties, mining claims remained inactive. With the arrival of the railroad in 1880, the boom was on.

One of the principal merchants of this era was Juan José Baca. Even before the railroad days, he had sent wagon trains to St. Louis, and now he prospered with the city. In the early 1880s, he enlarged his house and adjacent store and built this *portal* in front of them.

Porch Detail, Mills-Clegg House, Springer   36

The house was built in 1880 by a lawyer who had made a fortune on litigations in frontier towns and mining camps. As we have seen in plates 9 and 29, the design is transitional, combining two-story traditional porches with up-to-date jigsaw work. The details of the balustrade illustrate a similar fusion of elements: the beaded edge of the straight balusters was known in the Territory, but turned spindles, a Queen Anne motif, were very new. Also instructive is the way in which the surface of the post was animated by countersunk panels, by chamfered corners, and by moldings or shapes nailed to it.

37 Portal Details

The Spanish colonial tradition established the *portal* as the dominant external feature of the building. These *portales* generally followed a standard design, though the profile of a *zapata* might vary. In the hands of Territorial carpenters, however, there was no limit to the modification of forms. The turned posts (upper right) were probably produced commercially, and items like these undoubtedly inspired the carpenter who ornamented the posts shown adjacent to and below it. The neighborhood of Peñasco, whence these last examples derive, is particularly rich in post design. Starting with a six-inch square mill-cut post, carpenters created all kinds of variations, and since oil paint was also available, patterns were accentuated with color.

The post on the lower left, from Los Luceros, shows an earlier and more educated attempt to simulate a classical capital by means of applied moldings. The shaft is composed of three sections of two-inch joists, the end joists four inches wide, the center member six. A large view of the two-story porch is seen in plate 8.

38   Window, Tranquilino López House, Trampas

Window glass, brought across the prairie first by wagon and then by railroad, did more to change the appearance of New Mexico architecture than any other single factor. Early houses had been dark, lighted by small openings filled with waxed cloth or translucent selenite (a form of gypsum) or fitted with solid wooden shutters that were of no use in cold grey weather when one most needed daylight. No housewife who could afford it would put up with such primitive windows once glass became available. We know that this did not occur before the 1850s, as traders and soldiers in the area during the Mexican War repeatedly mentioned the absence of window glass. When it did arrive, however, windows were easy to cut or enlarge in old adobe buildings, as indicated by this window, installed perhaps as late as 1900 in a house that may date back to the 1820s.

One of the oldest and finest Territorial ranches in New Mexico was that of Samuel Watrous. His house, said to have been begun in 1849, was a traditional hacienda arranged around a *placita* and entered through a zaguan with double gates. (Rooms along one side of the courtyard have since disappeared.) At that early date, however, a house standing alone in the prairie would not have dared employ windows like these on the outside walls even if glass had been available. It is quite clear that the many windows and handsome wood trim that now distinguish the building date from a later remodeling, probably in the late 1860s. The brackets that support the cornice molding of the window frames are very like those seen on the center doors at Phoenix Ranch (plate 6), and both appear similar to details observed in old pictures of officers' quarters at Fort Union built in 1868. The ranches and the fort are within four miles of each other.

This picture also illustrates terneplate roofing (sheet iron coated with an alloy of tin and lead). This roofing came in panels about three feet long joined at standing seams. Tighter and longer lasting than board roofing, it was used by those who could afford it. Corrugated iron roofing, which comes in much larger sheets, was not available in New Mexico until after the completion of the railroad.

40   Windows, Church of San Francisco de Assisi, Ranchos de Taos

These large windows in the nave of the church are typical of later openings enlarged in or added to older buildings. The church, which did not exist when Fray Francisco Domínguez visited Taos in 1776, was probably constructed soon after the walled community of Ranchos de Taos was finished in 1779. It is safe to assume that these large windows were created when the main entrance of the church was remodeled into its present elaborate form by a carpenter whose name has not yet been discovered. (The same artisan must also have been responsible for the charming little Archuleta Oratorio in the La Loma district, just north of Taos.) The size of the glass and elaboration of the door trim suggest a fairly late date for the remodeling, perhaps in the 1880s.

Window trim like door design, was subject to fanciful variations. The pedimented lintel seen on the left derives from the gabled front of a classical temple. In the temple this was a functional element whose ridge roof covered an interior and shed water. Here, however, the pediment is reduced to the thickness of a single board and broken into four slopes, thereby losing any ability to shed water. Instead it has become a purely decorative shape, to be bent and elaborated as the carpenter's fancy dictates. The scrolled embellishment above the opening is cut from a board and nailed to the frame.

The other window comes from the Lucero store built in 1892 by Aniceto Garduño. Characteristic of his work is the series of small pendants below the window cornice. These pendants are built up by mitring and nailing sections of hand-planed moldings against the frame. The entrance to this store is seen in plate 22.

42   Bay Window, Hillsboro

Hillsboro, located in the Mimbres Mountains
west of the Rio Grande, was prevented even more
than Socorro from exploiting nearby silver and
gold deposits until Indian depredations were
halted by federal troops in the early 1880s. The
town then enjoyed a brief but vigorous boom,
only to wither within twenty years. Nevertheless, a
number of citified buildings were erected.

Cornice Detail, Mills-Clegg House, Springer   43

The window sash undivided by wooden muntins reflects the fashion for large expanses of glass then prevalent in the eastern part of the country. Obviously, however, it would have been hazardous to transport such large plates of glass by wagon.

The cornice projecting well beyond the wall was unknown in Territorial architecture, and it is additional evidence of American taste. The same is true of the paired brackets that support it, a feature used by eastern builders as early as the 1840s, during the Italianate movement. The photograph clearly shows that these heavy brackets are actually made up of five one-inch boards cut to the same profile and nailed together. The drops and the small, circular chips were also made separately and nailed on. It was much easier to compile decoration in this manner than to carve it from a single piece of wood. Other views of this house are found in plates 9, 29, and 36.

44 Fireplace, Hiram Long House, Ranchos de Taos

The most interesting architectural feature of a traditional New Mexico interior is undoubtedly the fogón—the fireplace. The standard design consists of a small fire chamber with an elliptical opening, placed in a corner. It stands on a low hearth that extends slightly into the room and is capped by a flat curved shelf. A small rectangular flue made of very thin (two-inch) adobes projects from the walls. Since the fire chamber is very small, logs must be short and are burned vertically, leaning against the back walls.

In situations where the builder wished to locate his fireplace nearer the center of the room rather than in one corner, he still constructed a corner fireplace by erecting a short parapet at right angles to the main wall and setting his fireplace against it. This small wall was called a *paredcito* ("little wall"), but in everyday speech the syllables are sometimes transposed to *padrecito* ("little father").

This fireplace, which heated Hiram Long's tavern room, probably dates from the 1840s. The remainder of the building has melted away, and this room is used as a cow barn. Long's zaguan gate is seen in plate 18.

Fireplace, Juan Ortega House, Chacón   45

A later date for this fireplace is indicated by the Yankee way of placing it parallel to the wall behind it rather than diagonally in a corner and by the use of wooden boards for the facing and the mantle shelf. It retains, however, the small fire box of traditional shape whose inside surfaces required frequent replastering. No kiln-burned bricks were made in the Territory until the late 1870s.

We are fortunate that this crude but charming hearth has survived, especially when one notices the plugged-up hole for the stovepipe at the top of the picture. Too often old fireplaces were demolished as being outmoded when more efficient iron stoves became available. In towns like Las Vegas and Albuquerque, where stoves were plentiful after the railroad was built, fireplaces were omitted from new homes, except for coal grates in the parlors of prosperous citizens; but in remote villages, where it was difficult to cart in stoves, fireplaces remained in use for a longer period.

46   Fireplace, José Valdez House, Taos

Possibly built as early as 1834, the José Gregorio Valdez house has the most unusual corner fireplace to survive in New Mexico. It is shaped like a large bell, hence the term *fogón de campana*. The hood is supported on two arches carried on a stumpy cylindrical pier, thus creating a hearth with two work areas. This may have been needed for a house as large as this one, which originally extended around a central *placita*. Today only three rooms are inhabited.

No other hearth like this has survived in New Mexico, but in the 1950s this design was copied for a fireplace in the Kit Carson Museum in Taos. The hard cement plaster is obviously modern and the level of the floor may have been raised, thereby eliminating the low hearth that is found in other early fireplaces.

Fireplace, Upper Morada, Arroyo Hondo   **47**

A corner fireplace of unusually large dimensions survives in a structure built as a morada and now converted to a house. As always, this morada had separate rooms for the chapel, never equipped with a fireplace or stove, and a meeting room that was heated. In this room the *hermanos* kept their Holy Week vigils, often of several days duration. Women brought in prepared meals, which were taken communally.

The small shelves to each side of the opening and the extensions of the hearth are unusual and may possibly have been used as places to keep pots of food warm. The walls here were originally covered with a white micaceous earth plaster. Other details of this building are seen in plates 13, 17, and 21.

48   Barns, Villanueva

Whereas dwellings in New Mexico were usually constructed of adobe, barns and storerooms were built of whatever material was readily available. In the mountain valleys, it was logs; in certain areas along the Pecos River or near Las Vegas, it was ledge stone; while in the Rio Grande Valley, adobe was preferred. Outcroppings near the town of Villanueva provided ledge stone, which was laid in adobe mortar. The corner section of this barn, however, appears to have been rebuilt with adobe.

Perched high on a hilltop overlooking the Pecos River, Villanueva is remarkably picturesque. When seen from the fields on the valley floor, it recalls an Italian hill town.

Corrals, Villanueva 49

Stone was also used for corral walls, though in later years board fencing was added. It is difficult to say whether the plastered houses in the middle ground are constructed of adobe or of stone covered with mud.

Almost every building in the town is roofed with corrugated iron, now rusted a deep reddish brown, though recent additions in the form of porches or new rooms can be distinguished by the lighter color of the roofing. Corrugated iron was introduced early to the community since it was easy to transport sheets of it from the Santa Fe Railroad only twelve miles away. The post and lintel construction equipped with a pulley to the left was undoubtedly used in butchering.

50   Trujillo Barn, Llano de San Juan

Typical of outbuildings on farms located close
to the high mountains is this hay barn built of logs.
The building was erected in two stages; the
section to the left, constructed of adzed logs, is
clearly the oldest. The second portion is made of
two-inch planking nailed on a framework of posts
and beams, a Yankee concept. Roofs of this kind,
uniform throughout and composed of two layers
of boards, were often built in areas where wood
was abundant and the railroad far away.

Hay Barn, Talpa   51

Animal pens and barns in mountain villages are usually constucted of logs faced on two sides but left rounded on the top and bottom; flat roofs are covered with strong vigas. Often hay is stacked on the roof, a solution that keeps the hay off the wet ground and provides a certain degree of insulation for the cattle stalls below.

52   Adobe Barn, Goke Ranch, Sapello

Because this barn is built into the side of a low hill, its right wall has been reinforced with a long benchlike buttress to minimize erosion at ground line. Though the walls are now surfaced with hard plaster, the soft plastic nature of adobe masonry is still expressed by the wavy lines of the corners and the buttress. Characteristic of this mountainous region also is the way the hayloft, situated under the ridge roof, is approached through a kind of dormer.

Storehouse, Manuel Atencio House, Trampas 53

In Trampas, outbuildings such as barns and animal shelters are constructed of logs, but since this structure was probably intended for the storage of grain or other edibles, it was constructed of adobe which could be tightly sealed. The roof line sweeps up gracefully at the corners and, with the warped profiles of the buttresses, creates a magnificent sculptural form. The silhouette is characteristic of the adobe structures in Trampas that

have not yet been covered with tin roofs. The adjacent Atencio residence is said to have been constructed in several campaigns between about 1820 and 1912.

Plaster in Trampas, as in Taos, is traditionally mixed with a good deal of straw, probably to facilitate drying. In the Rio Abajo, where the climate is drier, little if any straw is added.

54   Stable, Cassidy Residence and Store, Cleveland

Now used as a cow barn, this structure was built about 1895 as a stable, saddle room and tool room by Daniel Cassidy, who had acquired the adjacent store and house in 1891. Some of the outbuildings in the adjoining corral incorporate walls dating back to the early compound that is said to have constituted the first Spanish settlement in the Mora Valley.

The small windows of the lower story of the stable reflect the early custom of placing openings high and filling them with wooden bars. Although iron was no longer scarce when this structure was erected, the old method was followed, presumably from force of habit. The presence of such windows here illustrates a phenomenon often observed in architectural history: a solution used in a respectable building (a residence) in one era is employed by builders of a later generation for structures of a more utilitarian nature. In other words, architectural solutions tend in time to descend the social and economic ladder. The upper level of clapboards, nailed on a balloon frame construction and used for hay, was probably added when the adjacent store was enlarged in 1912.

Gristmill, Embudo Watershed   55

Gristmills constitute an interesting group of buildings in New Mexico and probably represent the first class of industrial buildings erected here. Once they were plentiful in the northern valleys, where water to power them was abundant. In the middle and southern Rio Grande Valley, animals were often used to turn the grinding stones until after the Civil War, when mills began to be driven by steam.

Though the oldest mills, like this one, were constructed of logs, their interiors were tightly sealed with adobe plaster. The mill wheel was placed horizontally and driven by a stream of water delivered at an angle by a hollowed-log chute. Such wheels in New Mexico rotate counter-clockwise, unlike Yankee wheels which are said to rotate clockwise.

56   St. Vrain Mill, Mora

Some of the later flour mills, like this one and the famous Aztec Mill of 1864 at Cimarron, were constructed of stone. Illustrated here is the mill erected for Ceran St. Vrain by Oliver Smith, which was already in operation by 1864. St. Vrain had gained fame as a soldier and merchant and big shareholder in the Mora Grant. He also owned a gristmill in Taos; that mill burned in August 1864.

This two-story stone mill with gambrel roof stood in the heart of the Mora Valley. The region was famous for its hard wheat, which made particularly good flour. Much of the flour ground at this mill in its early days was sold to nearby Fort Union or to agents who contracted with the federal government to furnish food for Indians.

Rather similar in appearance to mills found in the Midwest is this board and batten structure in Vadito. It was erected about 1875 and operated until 1922. The board sheathing retains marks of the circular saws with which it was cut, but the stones in the foundation were laid in a mortar of mud. The bark-boarded shed at the left is a recent addition.

As in most mountain mills water to turn the wheel for this mill came from the same ditch that irrigated fields farther down the valley. Millponds were seldom if ever constructed in New Mexico; when the supply of ditchwater was insufficient, one merely postponed grinding.

Only one mill is now in operation in the entire Embudo watershed, where perhaps as many as two dozen once worked. The surviving mill, a small log building constructed about 1870 by Acorcino Cordova, is at Rockwall.

58   Cleveland Flour Mill, Cleveland

Constructed of adobe on a well-laid stone foundation, the Cleveland Flour Mill was erected in 1877 by Joseph Fuss, retooled in 1893, and acquired by Daniel Cassidy in 1914. The first buhrstones were imported from France, but the present roller mill was installed in 1892, when the large waterwheel of metal was added. The mill remained in operation until 1950, after which time the declining agriculture of the valley could no longer provide sufficient grain. Since the machinery of the mill is still intact, there is talk of operating again with imported wheat.

The large vertical waterwheel (diameter 18 feet 6 inches), which was constructed of prefabricated iron parts and assembled on the site, is located at the opposite end of the structure from that pictured here. Sections of the wall near the wheel and millrace are of stone set in cement mortar.

This is one of the oldest mill sites in the area. The first structure here was built in 1850 by Vicente Romero, whose hacienda stood a short distance away (plate 7). The present structure, with stone foundations, shingle roof, and Territorial trim, probably dates from the mid-seventies. The mill's prosperity outlasted Fort Union, for which it was chief supplier of flour, and it was fitted with new grinding equipment as recently as 1920.

The Territorial trim of the store building adjacent to the mill is distinctive because of the pronounced projections of the cornices capping the windows and doors. The segmental arch of the window makes a curious contrast with the horizontal window head. The presence of an earlier loading platform is indicated by an eroded zone on the adobe wall.

60 Apse Elevation, Church of San José, Trampas

A paradigm of the colonial New Mexican church, this structure was erected between 1760, when permission to build it was granted by Bishop Tamarón of Durango, Mexico, and 1776, when Fray Francisco Domínguez reported that only a few details remained to be completed. From that date to the present the church remained almost unchanged because the village was isolated and so poor that it could afford neither modernization nor the equally disastrous restoration that has beset most other missions in New Mexico. The undulating walls and sharp angles of the silhouette are characteristic of Trampas buildings (see plate 53), and the church is still plastered with adobe. Plastering must be repeated every six to eight years; it last took place here in 1964. Trampas is the last large church in the region still covered

with this beautiful material. In 1964, too, delicate wooden belfries were added on the facade to replace the similar towers seen in old photographs. Such towers, however, could hardly have been added before 1880.

The cruciform plan of this structure was sometimes used for churches in Spanish communities in eighteenth-century New Mexico, whereas during the previous century single-aisle churches had been the rule. This change in plan reflected practice in Mexico where, from the late seventeenth century on, parish churches were built in a cross shape with a dome at the crossing. Another characteristic is the absence of fenestration. Even though there are only six windows in the church today, each of the present openings is several times larger than the original.

Erected as a private chapel by Bernardo Abeyta by 1816, this building shows how little church design in New Mexico changed in two centuries. It retains the single-aisle, polygonal apse plan, and the transverse clerestory used as early as 1626 in the church at Isleta Pueblo. The church was originally a traditional flat-roof structure with an elevated apse, but its appearance was drastically changed when a corrugated iron roof was added during World War I. Wooden ornaments and gables were added to the twin towers at the same time. In contrast to the soft shapes and horizontal lines of the original building, the additions reflect the rather medieval style introduced into New Mexico architecture in 1869 when Bishop Lamy began construction of the Cathedral of St. Francis in Santa Fe.

The window in the recessed gallery above the front door is of unusual interest as a reminder of the region's early fenestration. A gridiron frame is constructed with closely spaced spindles arranged in a vertical position. Even though such a window would not open, solid inside shutters are provided for additional protection. Although the window now contains narrow panes of glass fixed between spindles grooved to receive them, the spaces originally were filled with pieces of selenite.

62   Chapel of the Assumption, Placitas

Typical of the small churches built in villages settled in the nineteenth century is that of Placitas, a community on the northern edge of the Embudo watershed. This building, like those in the nearby villages of Vadito and Rodarte, contains a rounded apse rather than the usual polygonal shape employed in larger churches. The original flat roof packed with earth exists below the modern cover-

ing of corrugated iron with its incongruous wooden gable. The presence of the old roof can be detected by the round vigas cut flush with the surface of the adobe wall. The double doors exemplify the folk art of the latter part of the century. The facade buttresses are probably original, constructed to secure the building on its hillside site.

Morada, Llano de San Juan (Nepomoceno)   63

A morada is ordinarily found on the edge of or even at some distance from the community in which the *hermanos* live, and a cemetery is usually adjacent to it. Almost always a large cross, the *Calvario,* stands nearby. Small windows, generally with shutters, indicate the brothers' desire for privacy.

Weeds grow from the earth that covers the roof of the building. *Canales* throw rainwater away from the adobe walls. The covering of hard plaster was added in 1965.

64   Morada, Rodarte

A morada cannot be identified by its appearance alone. Moradas were built of whatever material was available locally; some show recent additions of concrete block. The sanctuary end can be round, as in plate 63, or rectangular, and roofs are either pitched or flat.

A morada has a minimum of two rooms: one a chapel or oratory, the second a meeting room with its fireplace or stove (plate 47). A larger morada may include a room for storage and even one for records.

In the structure shown here the wood gable and corrugated iron roof are clearly more recent additions, but the small, irregularly placed windows are part of the original building. The characteristic free-standing cross is seen at the right, while a log storage-building, detached from the two-room morada, can be observed in the background.

Old Church of Santa Gertrudis, Mora   65

Although an outpost was established in Mora as early as 1835, this building is said to be the first church edifice erected there. Now used by the parish as a center for youth activities, this structure has been superseded by two successive church buildings, the latest of which was dedicated in 1972.

The building is a simple but rather handsome piece of architecture. The recessed porch is somewhat reminiscent of the temple *in antis* form used by Greek Revival designers, and the proportions and workmanship of the wood frame and doors of the entrance are not inferior to those of the Presbyterian church in Las Vegas (plate 24). On the other hand, the simple window trim and the wooden gable above the adobe building are visually quite similar to the two-story Mora County Courthouse, long since destroyed but seen in a photograph said to date from 1860.

66 Chapel, Los Luceros

Dedicated to the Holy Family this chapel was built in thanksgiving by the Luis Ortiz family for the deliverance of its nearby mansion (plate 8) from the flooding Rio Grande, probably during the flood of 1886 that destroyed the old church at Santo Domingo Pueblo. The donors of the chapel, who are said to be buried under the floor, deeded the chapel to the archbishop in 1890.

The most salient external feature of the chapel today is the splendid double doors. They were not, however, part of the original building, for they long graced Policarpio Romero's house in Peñasco (plate 28). They are among the finest surviving products of the traditional folk art that once flourished in New Mexico.

An interesting feature here is the way the roof steps up at the altar end of the chapel (barely visible at the right edge of the illustration). Although the chapel was designed to have a ridge roof, thus eliminating the possibility of a transverse clerestory window illuminating the interior, the tradition of a raised apse ceiling was so strong that the builders adhered to it.

67　Descanso, Peñas Negras Cemetery, near Taos

This little cemetery occupies a hillside location on the west bank of Taos River about two miles north of Las Cordovas, which it serves. As there was no church or morada, a shelter was constructed where a coffin could rest while the grave was prepared. It is not a chapel, for it contains no altar; such buildings are not common in New Mexico.

The only architectural accent is the charming bit of wooden trim, cut with a jigsaw. Its design is identical to that used on the *portal* of the Leandro

Martínez house that once stood a mile and a half upstream. Martínez's house was built in 1862, and the owner was reported by a descendant to have been his own carpenter. Undoubtedly, he also did the carpentry on this *descanso*. The present frieze, however, is a replacement, added in about 1955. Unprotected by paint or preservative, the original frieze had fallen off, but enough remained to serve as a model when a citizen of Taos, regretting the decay, commissioned the repairs.

Gateway, Romero Family Cemetery, Chacón   68

On a hillside overlooking the Chacón Valley is another cemetery without chapel, morada, or even a *descanso*. Other than the stone wall and a few fenced graves, the only architectural accent is the gateway. Worked out with lattice and a few bits of molding, the staged tower resembles the belfries that were used for churches of the period. It is not unlike the nineteenth-century towers of wood added to Trampas (plate 60). The little spot of ornament at the apex of the triangular opening, a simple square made by mitring four pieces of molding, has the unmistakable touch of Aniceto Garduño, who did so much work in the area. Details identical to this are found on frames of the sacristy door and window of Capilla de San Antonio in Chacón.

69　Romero Family Cemetery, Chacón

During the second phase of the Territorial style, wooden pickets were often used to form railings around graves. The balusters were often cut with an intricate profile, while a higher, more elaborate piece formed a cross at the head of the grave. The components of each grave were slightly different, and the cross sometimes flowered into a very complicated shape. Such wooden fences were undoubtedly rural reflections of the intricate cast iron railings placed around graves in the East and Midwest during the middle decades of the nineteenth century. While such iron barriers were sometimes used in Santa Fe or Las Vegas, they were undoubtedly too costly for villagers.

Grave Marker, Galisteo   70

Like fancy window and door trim, grave markers and fencing were made by village carpenters and show infinite variation. Almost always unpainted, the wood eventually took on a patina and weather-beaten texture, often eroded by blowing sand. Sometimes, however, an inscription would be painted on the headboard. Where it was thus protected, the surface did not wear away as rapidly and retains a blurred and ghostly bas relief.

GLOSSARY

adobe: brick of sun-dried earth and straw

aedicule: a niche for a statue

baluster: a short support like a column

balustrade: a row of balusters topped by a rail

canal: waterspout

chamfer: to cut off corners or edges

clerestory: an outside wall above an adjoining roof, pierced with windows which admit light to the interior

corbel: a member which projects from within a wall and supports a superincumbent weight

cornice: the projecting horizontal member that crowns an architectural composition

corral: a yard or enclosure

dentil: a small block in a series projecting like teeth (as under the corona of a cornice)

descanso: a shelter where a coffin could be placed while the grave was prepared

entablature: an architecturally treated wall resting on columns and supporting the pediment or roof

fogón: a corner-set fireplace

miter: to bring together at an angle without overlapping

morada: a Penitente chapel

muntin: a strip separating panes of glass with a sash

ogee: a molding with a S-shaped profile

oratorio: private chapel

pintle: a pivot pin on which another part turns

placita: a small plaza serving a complex of buildings or located in the center of a private home

plaza: public square

portal: long porch or portico with roof supported by vertical posts and corbels

portico: a colonnade, usually at the entrance of a building

reveal: the side of an opening between a doorframe and the outer surface of a wall

soffit: the underside of a part of a building

tenon: a projecting member for insertion into a mortise to make a joint

terneplate: sheet iron or steel coated with an alloy of tin and lead

viga: ceiling beam

yeso: gypsum

zaguan: roofed space joining separate buildings or rooms

zapata: corbeled impost